The Sun

Written by
Paulette Bourgeois

Illustrated by
Bill Slavin

Kids Can Press

Acknowledgments

I am grateful for the help of the scientists at the McLaughlin Planetarium at the Royal Ontario Museum, and the Ontario Science Centre for sending information and answering questions. I am thankful that Terence Dickinson, a man who knows more about the skies than almost anyone else, made the time to read my manuscripts and make helpful suggestions. Bill Slavin was very patient and did a spectacular job making the science come alive. And finally, I would like to thank Elizabeth MacLeod, a wonderful writer and editor, who always asked the right questions and kept me on track.

First U.S. edition 1997

Published in Canada by
Kids Can Press Ltd.
29 Birch Avenue
Toronto, ON M4V 1E2

Published in the U.S. by
Kids Can Press Ltd.
85 River Rock Drive, Suite 202
Buffalo, NY 14207

CMC 95 09876543
CMC PA 96 098765432

A story about the Sun's energy, page 33, adapted from Tcakabesh Snares the Sun, from THE MAN IN THE MOON by Alta Jablow and Carl Withers. Copyright © 1969 by Alta Jablow and Carl Withers. Illustrations copyright © 1969 by Peggy Wilson. Reprinted by permission of Henry Holt and Co., Inc.

Photo Credits
Bill Ivy: page 8, 14, 16, 17, 18, 24, 26, 28, 30, 32, 34, 37.
NASA: page 4, 6, 22, 31, 38

Canadian Cataloguing in Publication Data
Bourgeois, Paulette
    The sun

(Starting with space)
Includes index.
ISBN 1-55074-158-6 (bound)
ISBN 1-55074-330-9 (pbk.)

1. Sun — Juvenile literature. 2. Sun — Experiments — Juvenile literature. I. Slavin, Bill. II. Title. III. Series.

QB521.5.B67 1995   j523.7   C95-930757-5

Edited by Elizabeth MacLeod
Text design by Marie Bartholomew
Page layout and cover design by Esperança Melo
Printed in Hong Kong by Wing King Tong Co. Ltd.

Contents

The Sun: Earth's star

Ancient people knew the Sun brought light and warmth. But they didn't know what made it shine and where it went each night. So they made up stories to help them understand the secrets of the Sun.

Sun tales

Long ago, the Egyptians thought the sky goddess, Nut, swallowed the Sun every night and gave birth to a new Sun the next morning.

People in Lithuania in eastern Europe told a different story. The Sun and Moon fell in love and got married. They had a baby and named her Earth. But the parents were always fighting. The Moon told the Sun to stop being so hot. The Sun told the Moon to stop being cold. They decided to separate.

If you see a word you don't know, look it up in the glossary on page 39.

But they both wanted to keep Earth. When they couldn't decide what to do, they visited the great god Thunder. Thunder told the Sun to take care of her daughter from morning until night and told the Moon to take care of Earth during the night.

And that's the way it's always been. Once in a while, when the Moon is too busy, his sisters, the stars, shine on Earth.

What is the Sun?

The Sun is a star — a bright, big ball of burning gas. It seems much larger than any other star because it is so much closer. The Sun is 150 million km (93 million miles) away from Earth. That seems like a long way but if the Sun were closer, nothing on Earth could survive the heat.

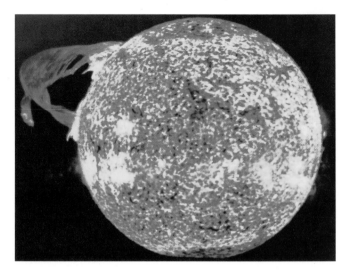

Here is one of the biggest solar flares ever.

SUN FACTS

The Sun measures 1 392 000 km (865 000 miles) across. If the Sun were an empty ball you could fit one million Earths inside it.

The Sun weighs 2 billion billion billion t (tons). That's 2 with 27 zeros after it. That's 333 000 times as much as Earth!

20000000000000000000000000000

The Sun's gravity is 28 times greater than Earth's. If you weigh 45 kg (100 pounds) on Earth, you'd weigh almost 1.5 t (tons) on the Sun!

The Sun is 4½ billion years old.

How big a star is the Sun?

The Sun is a medium-sized star. Scientists say stars come in all sizes — anywhere from dwarf to giant size. They can be almost as small as Earth or 40 times as big as the Sun. Stars can glow blue (which means they are very hot), white, yellow or red (much cooler). Scientists call our Sun a yellow dwarf.

What does the Sun do?

The Sun gives us light and heat. The Sun's light makes plants grow. Plants give us food to eat and oxygen to breathe. We would die without them.

The Sun's heat gives us rain. When the Sun warms lakes and oceans some of the water changes into a gas called water vapor. This gas floats high in the sky to where the air is cooler. The water vapor is chilled and changes back into water drops. When a lot of these drops join together, they form clouds. If the water drops get large enough, they fall as rain.

The Sun's heat also gives us wind. The heat warms the air and when air is warm, it moves. And wind is moving air.

If there were no Sun, Earth would have no wind, rain, heat or light.

When did the Sun start to shine?
The Sun started to shine 4½ billion years ago.

Long, long before that, there were nothing but gases floating around in the universe. About 12 billion years ago, pockets of gas gathered together to form the Milky Way galaxy. Over time, hundreds of billions of stars were born inside the Milky Way.

Our Sun was one of those stars. It started as an enormous cool cloud of gas and dust. It became smaller and hotter until it started to shine.

Will the Sun shine forever?

No, all stars die. In about 5 billion years the Sun will start to glow red and grow bigger. It will become so hot that the ice at Earth's North Pole will melt and the oceans will begin to boil. The Sun will continue to grow until it swallows the planets closest to it — including Earth! Then the Sun will begin to shrink and become dimmer and dimmer until it is a small, dim star called a white dwarf.

Sun stuff

The solar system is the name given to the Sun and everything that travels around it, including the planets and their moons. Solar means "about the sun."

Why does the Sun shine?
It all starts in the Sun's center, also known as its core. The Sun's core is super hot, hotter than any furnace on Earth. And all the weight of the huge, heavy Sun presses on its core. The Sun is mostly made of hydrogen gas and near the core that gas becomes super hot and super squished. That makes the hydrogen turn into helium gas and give off huge blasts of energy as it changes.

Every second, 4 million tons of hydrogen change into helium and energy. But don't worry about the Sun using up all its hydrogen.

There is enough hydrogen in the Sun to keep it shining for another 5 billion years.

The energy the Sun makes as the hydrogen changes to helium starts moving from the Sun's core toward the outside. But because the Sun is so large and heavy, it takes millions of years for the energy to pass through it. When the energy finally reaches the Sun's surface, some of it turns into waves of light and heat that move outward very quickly through the emptiness of space. On Earth you can see the Sun's light waves, or sunshine, and you can feel the heat waves.

Sun stuff

Light takes only 8 minutes and 20 seconds to zoom from the Sun to Earth. The fastest jet on Earth would take a million times that long. Some stars you see at night are so far away that their light takes 4000 years to reach us!

The Sun gives off many types of energy waves besides light waves and heat waves but you can't see or feel any of them.

What does the Sun look like?

You should never look at the Sun, not even with strong sunglasses. Your eyes focus the Sun's light onto a small spot inside them. That makes the light strong enough to burn your eyes and make you blind. However, scientists have machines that let them look at the Sun so they can see its different parts.

Chromosphere — a layer of gas. The Sun's brightness makes it hard to see.

Photosphere — the part of the Sun that shines. It looks like boiling lava up close.

Corona — a layer of very hot gas

Flares — a super powerful burst of energy

Sunspots — cooler spots on the Sun. Some are bigger than the Earth.

Prominences — ribbons of gas that loop far into space and back to the Sun

The parts of the Sun

TRY IT!
Look at the Sun safely

You'll need:
- a sunny day
- tape
- a large piece of white paper
- a small square of cardboard
- a small nail
- a stake or stick
- a bucket of sand
- a mirror
- an adult helper

1. Tape the paper to a wall outside.

2. Have an adult punch a hole in the center of the cardboard with the nail. Tape the cardboard to the stick — don't put the hole in front of the stick!

3. Stand the stick in the bucket of sand. Place the bucket in front of the paper on the wall.

4. Ask a friend to hold the mirror and move it until it reflects the Sun through the hole in the cardboard. Look at the white paper until you see an image of the Sun. Draw what you see.

Looking at the Sun this way is a safe way to get an idea of how the Sun looks. Did you see any dark spots on the Sun? These are sunspots. Repeat this project a few days later and compare your pictures. You'll see that not all the sunspots are in the same place in both pictures. That's because sunspots move as the Sun spins.

Following the Sun

Long ago, people kept track of the seasons by
following the Sun.
They knew that in summer the Sun was high in the sky.
In winter it was much lower.
By watching the Sun, people knew when to gather food
for winter or to prepare for yearly rains or droughts.
And they all told stories about why there are seasons.

A story about the seasons

In ancient Greek stories, a beautiful goddess named Demeter looked after Earth. She especially loved harvest time, while her daughter, Persephone, loved the flowers of spring.

Below the surface of the Earth lived a god named Hades. His land was dark and gloomy. He kidnapped Persephone because he wanted her brightness to light his world. Demeter missed her daughter so much that she stopped caring for Earth. It began to dry up. Plants died and people were starving.

Demeter told the gods she could not look after Earth until her daughter came home. So Zeus, the father of the heavens, told Hades to return Persephone to her mother. But Zeus had one rule. If Persephone had eaten any food from the underworld, she could not return.

When Demeter saw her daughter again she was so happy that flowers bloomed. Then the sad truth came out. Persephone had eaten four pomegranate seeds while with Hades. She must go back to him. That meant Earth would die, and Zeus could not bear that. He decided Persephone would live with Hades for four months each year, one month for every seed.

Ever since, Earth is cold and dark while Persephone is away from Demeter. But as soon as she returns, there are spring flowers and sunshine. Mother and daughter spend summer together but as the time comes for Persephone to leave, plants start to die and Earth gets colder.

Why do we have seasons?

When it's summer where you live, the Sun is shining almost directly on you. The weather turns cold when the Sun's light shines on you from an angle. Then you get winter.

The seasons change because Earth leans to one side as it orbits, or circles, the Sun. As Earth makes one complete orbit around the Sun, your part of the world is either leaning toward the Sun or away from the Sun. People who live near the equator do not have seasons because they always get almost direct rays from the Sun.

When it is winter in the Northern hemisphere, it is summer in the Southern hemisphere.

The path a planet takes around the Sun is called its orbit. Earth takes 1 year, or 365 days and 6 hours, to make 1 orbit. Every 4 years those extra hours add up to a whole day and that day is added to the end of February. This special 366-day year is called a leap year.

What is a solstice?

A solstice takes place twice a year when the midday Sun is as low or as high in the sky as it can be. One solstice happens around December 21 and, north of the equator, it's known as the winter solstice. The other solstice takes place around June 21 and is called the summer solstice in the Northern hemisphere.

On the winter solstice, your part of the world is leaning as far away from the Sun as possible. This is known as the shortest day of the year because there are fewer hours of daylight than on any other day.

At the summer solstice, your part of the world leans as close to the Sun as possible. On that day you receive more hours of daylight than any other day. It's known as the longest day of the year. When it is the winter solstice in the Northern hemisphere, it is the summer solstice in the Southern hemisphere.

The first day of spring or fall is called the equinox. On these days, there are 12 hours of daylight and 12 hours of night.

Why do we have day and night?

If it is day where you live, your part of the world is facing the Sun. When night falls, your part of the world faces away from the Sun. This happens because every 24 hours Earth spins — or rotates — like a slowly spinning top. Half of the world is in sunlight while the other half is in darkness.

> The Sun rises in the eastern part of the sky and sets in the west. At noon, your shadow points north if you are above the equator and south if you are below it.

During the summer the Sun is higher in the sky than it is in winter. The time between sunrise and sunset is longer, too. If you lived near the North Pole, you would see the Sun all night and all day in the middle of summer and you wouldn't see the Sun at all in the middle of winter.

At sunrise, your part of the world is beginning to face the Sun.

TRY IT!
Cast a big shadow

Plan to start this project early in the morning. You'll need to come back to spend a few minutes with it throughout the day.

> **You'll need:**
> ○ a sunny day
> ○ a large, open space such as a school yard
> ○ a friend
> ○ a piece of chalk
> ○ a measuring tape or measuring stick

1. In the early morning, ask your friend to stand in a sunny place. Trace around your friend's shadow. Measure the length of the shadow. Make a note of the time you do this.

2. Repeat step 1 about every two hours until late in the day.

3. Look at your shadow pictures and measurements. When is the shadow the longest?

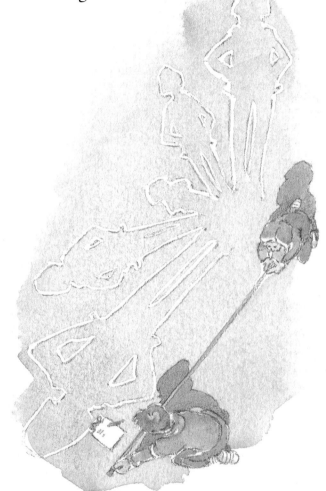

You should observe that your friend's shadow is shortest in the middle of the day and longest near sunrise and sunset.

Try this project again in a different season. You'll find that the shadow is shortest in summer because the Sun is highest in the sky.

What is a sundial?

A sundial is a clock that uses the Sun to tell time. The pointer on the sundial casts a shadow onto a disk that has lines marked on it. These markings each have a time of day written beside them. As the Earth turns, throughout the day, the pointer's shadow moves across the disk. If the shadow falls on the line marked 11, then it is 11:00 in the morning.

The early Egyptians were the first people to discover how to use the Sun to tell time. Their sundials, or shadow clocks, were made of just a stick stuck in the ground, with lines scratched in the earth around it.

The stick is called a gnomon (say it NO-MUN) from the Greek word meaning "one who knows."

TRY IT!
Make your own sundial

Start this project early in the morning. You'll need to spend a few minutes with it every hour throughout the day.

You'll need:
- a sunny day
- an open sunny place
- a small ball of Plasticine
- a piece of cardboard about 25 cm x 25 cm (10 inches x 10 inches)
- a small stick
- a watch
- a pencil

1. Place the Plasticine in the middle of one of the edges of the cardboard.

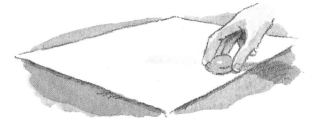

2. Stand the stick straight up in the middle of Plasticine as shown.

3. Put your sundial in a sunny place so that the stick's shadow falls on the cardboard.

4. Mark the spot where the shadow falls on your cardboard. Write down the time beside it. Your sundial will be easier to use if you mark the shadow's position on the hour. Do this every hour until the Sun goes down.

If you leave your sundial where it is, you can use it to tell time on any sunny day. If the stick's shadow is between your marks, you can tell the time by deciding which of the marks the shadow is closer to. You'll probably quickly discover why people now use clocks instead of sundials. Sundials can't tell time at night or on cloudy days.

The astronauts on the *Apollo 12* spacecraft took this picture of a solar eclipse.

What is an eclipse?

Imagine you're outside on a clear, sunny day. Suddenly the sky begins to turn dark. There's a dark hole on one side of the Sun and the hole is getting bigger! Soon all that is left of the Sun is a halo of sparkling light around a black circle. On Earth the sky is as dark as twilight. The birds are silent and the air feels colder. There is an eerie quiet.

Is the Sun dying? No — an eclipse is taking place. Sometimes the Sun, Moon and Earth line up in a straight line with the Moon in the middle. The Moon blocks the Sun's light from reaching Earth and a solar eclipse occurs.

If the Moon blocks all the Sun's light, it causes a total eclipse of the Sun. When only part of the Sun's light is blocked, a partial eclipse of the Sun takes place. As the Earth and Moon continue in their orbits and move out of line, more and more sunlight appears. The eclipse is over.

BE CAREFUL! IT IS NEVER SAFE TO LOOK AT THE SUN, EVEN DURING AN ECLIPSE.

When is the next eclipse?

There are usually two to four solar eclipses each year. You'll experience a total eclipse only if where you live is completely in the Moon's shadow.

Date	Where eclipse will be seen
August 11, 1999	Atlantic Ocean, England, France, Turkey, India
June 21, 2001	Brazil, Africa, south Atlantic ocean
December 4, 2002	Africa, western Australia

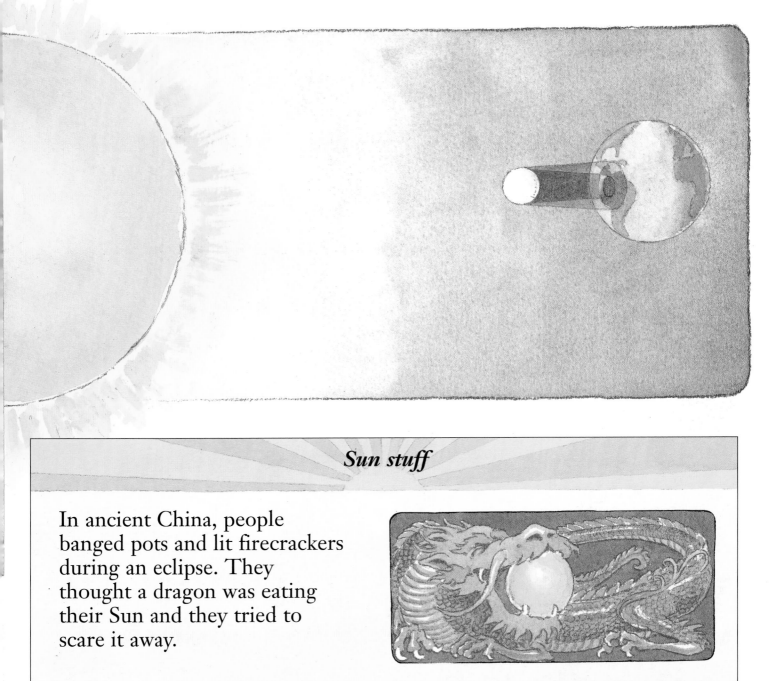

Sun stuff

In ancient China, people banged pots and lit firecrackers during an eclipse. They thought a dragon was eating their Sun and they tried to scare it away.

The Sun's light

What color is sunlight?
You may think it's yellow, but in this chapter you'll
find out that's only part of the answer.
You'll also discover how the Sun's light makes rainbows.
The Shoshone People of the northwestern
United States tell this story to explain the appearance
of the first rainbow.

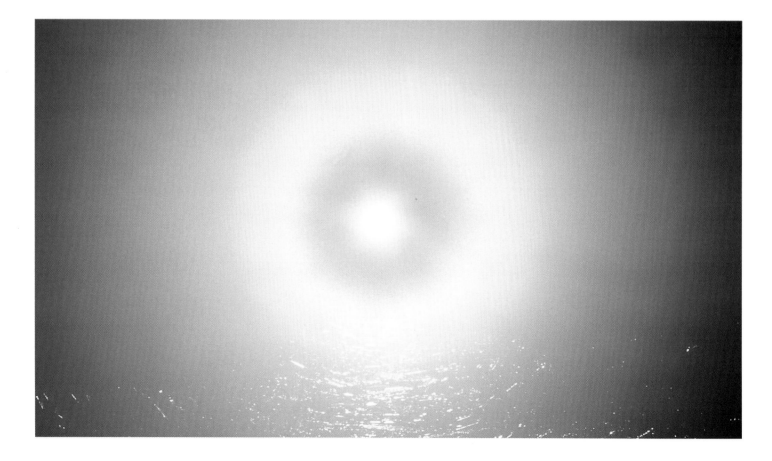

How the sky got a rainbow

When you look at a rainbow, does it remind you of a snake? Long ago, a Shoshone storyteller imagined just that. He told of a time when there was no rain,

and the people had no food or water. A magical snake told them to throw him into the air. What could a snake do? the people wondered. The snake begged them again to throw him into the air. Finally, a shaman, a man with magical powers, threw the snake upward. The snake stretched until he reached across the sky.

Then he arched his back and changed from one color to another.

The snake rubbed his scales against the sky until rain fell from the clouds. When the rains were done, the people danced with joy and the Sun started to shine again. Now whenever the Sun shines after a rain, the snake comes out to show his colors.

What color is sunlight?

The sunlight you see every day looks white but it is really a mixture of seven different colors: red, orange, yellow, green, blue, indigo and violet. The colors are always the same and they are always arranged in the same order.

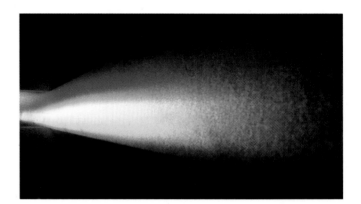

How can you see all the colors in sunlight?

You can only see all the colors when sunlight is split up. One way this happens is when sunlight shines through glass cut into a special shape called a prism.

Light slows down when it goes through a prism and changes direction. Another way to say this is that light bends or refracts. Violet — the color that travels the slowest — makes the sharpest change in direction. Red travels the fastest and makes a small change in direction.

TRY IT!

Make a rainbow

What you see is a rainbow — all the colors in light. How are rainbows formed in the sky? After a rain there are raindrops still in the air. Each raindrop acts as a prism splitting the light into all its colors. If you're standing with the Sun behind you and air with lots of water drops in it (such as just after a rain) in front of you, you will see a rainbow.

1. Put the prism or other crystal where the sun will shine on it.

2. Hold the paper as shown so that the light coming through the prism hits the paper. What do you see on the paper?

Why is the sky blue and a sunset red?

When the Sun is high in the sky during the day, the blue light in the sunlight is scattered by particles in Earth's air and the sky looks blue. When the Sun is low in the sky at sunset, more of the other colors are scattered too, and the sky becomes more colorful.

After a volcano erupts you'll see redder sunsets because there is more dust and ash in the air to scatter the red light.

This setting Sun isn't really red — the air scatters the other colors of light more easily so that only the red light in sunlight gets through when the Sun is near the horizon.

TRY IT!

Find out why sunsets are red

You'll need:
- ○ a dark room
- ○ a table
- ○ a clear bowl
- ○ water
- ○ an eyedropper or spoon
- ○ milk
- ○ a flashlight
- ○ a piece of white paper

1. Fill the bowl with water. Add a few drops of milk until the water seems cloudy.

2. Hold the white paper as shown behind the bowl.

3. Hold the flashlight so that the light shines through the milky water and reflects on the white paper. What colors do you see on the paper?

You should see a reddish color like the color of a sunset. The milk in the water scatters the light just as the gases in the atmosphere scatter light.

What is UV light?

UV, or ultraviolet light, is invisible light from the Sun. Most UV light is absorbed by a gas in Earth's atmosphere called ozone. But some passes through. This UV light gives your skin a tan by making it produce a brown chemical called melanin. Too much UV light can give you a sunburn and harm plants and animals.

What is the ozone layer?

About 40 km (25 miles) above Earth there is a thin layer of a gas called ozone. One of the most important things ozone does is stop too much UV light from reaching Earth.

Chemicals known as chlorofluorocarbons, or CFCs, eat up ozone. CFCs get into the atmosphere when refrigerators and air conditioners are destroyed. Around the world there are laws to cut down on the use of CFCs and keep the ozone layer safe.

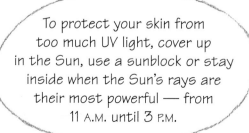

Ozone

Ultraviolet

To protect your skin from too much UV light, cover up in the Sun, use a sunblock or stay inside when the Sun's rays are their most powerful — from 11 A.M. until 3 P.M.

What are the northern lights?

The northern lights are the colorful, dancing bands of light that appear in the night sky over countries such as Canada that are close to the North Pole. They are also called the *aurora borealis*.

The auroras are caused by a weird wind called a solar wind. Every second, many tons of bits of the Sun are blown into space, forming a wind of small particles moving away from the Sun. Near the Earth, some of these particles are trapped by an invisible shield called the Earth's magnetic field.

The magnetic field pulls the particles toward the North and South poles. As they are pulled lower and lower, they light up gases in Earth's atmosphere and you see beautiful dancing lights.

Sun stuff

Near the South Pole the colorful bands of lights are called the southern lights or *aurora australis*.

Astronauts on the space shuttle *Discovery* took this picture of the *aurora borealis*.

Using the Sun's energy

The Sun gives us more than light. We can use the Sun's energy for power and it also keeps us warm. The Algonkian people of Canada tell a legend that warns about the hot, hot heat of the Sun.

A story about the Sun's energy

Tcakabesh lived with his sister in the forest where he hunted and fished for food.

One day he went to the place where the Earth meets the sky to lay a trap to catch some supper.

The next day the Sun did not rise.

"Go and see what has happened to the Sun," said his sister.

Tcakabesh hurried to the place where the Sun meets the sky. There, inside his trap, was the Sun! Tcakabesh tried to free it, but he couldn't get close because the Sun was too hot. He asked all the animals to help. "If we do not," he pleaded, "there will always be darkness."

The animals tried, one after the other, to free the Sun. The squirrel tried to bite the ropes, but the Sun was too hot. It made the squirrel's tail turn up at the end and it is still that way.

Finally, the mouse tried. He nibbled right through the ropes. The hair on his back was singed off and it is still that way. But the mouse freed the Sun. The Sun rose into the sky and was never trapped again.

What are heat rays?

Heat rays are just one of the many kinds of rays that come from the Sun. You can feel them when you stand in sunlight. They make your skin feel warm.

We only feel a tiny part of all the heat rays the Sun sends out. That's a good thing — if all the Sun's heat rays hit Earth, everything would burn up!

Why do some things get hotter in the Sun than others?

Everything heats up at different speeds.
Air heats up faster than water — that's why you can take a cool dip in a pool on a hot day. Light colors reflect heat, so they stay cooler and dark colors absorb heat, so they stay warmer. Shiny, smooth surfaces also reflect heat, while rough, dull surfaces keep heat in.

TRY IT!
Find the warmest color

You'll need:
- a sunny day
- five ice cubes
- squares of colored paper in black, white, red, blue and yellow
- a clock or watch

1. Put an ice cube in the center of each piece of paper.

2. Time how long it takes each ice cube to melt. Which one melts the fastest?

You want to wear a jacket made from a color that absorbs the most heat. The faster an ice cube melts, the more heat the paper it is on absorbs. Which color absorbs heat the fastest? Which absorbs heat the slowest?

A jacket made from a dark fabric absorbs more heat and will keep you warmer.

What is solar power?

Solar power is power we get from the Sun. We use the Sun's energy to warm buildings, heat water and make electricity.

One way we gather the Sun's energy is in solar panels — black boxes with glass tops. (You already found out on page 35 how well black absorbs light.) You can see these boxes on the roofs of buildings. Water flowing through the solar panels is warmed by the Sun. That warm water then runs through pipes in the building to keep the rooms warm.

Solar cells are another way we use the Sun's power. They turn the Sun's light into electricity to power watches, calculators and even space satellites. Solar power will become even more important in the future as we use up fuels such as wood, coal and oil.

How do plants use the Sun?

Plants use sunlight to make food. When the Sun shines on green plants, it starts a process in their leaves that creates food. While plants make food they take in carbon dioxide gas and breathe out oxygen. You breathe in oxygen and breathe out carbon dioxide. So plants and people depend on each other and we all depend on the Sun.

You can tell plants need the Sun — watch how they turn toward it!

Sun stuff

Plants make food in their leaves using mostly air, water and the Sun's light. This food-making process is called photosynthesis. *Photo* comes from the Greek word for light.

Why study the Sun?

People have always been fascinated by the Sun. The Mayan Indians, who lived long ago in Mexico and Central America, built huge observatories so they could follow it and find out more about the glowing ball they depended on.

Scientists today study the Sun so they can discover more about how it shines with such a steady light.

In 1976 a solar probe called *Helios 2* came closer to the Sun than any spacecraft ever had. It came within 45 million km (28 million miles) of the Sun — any closer and it would have fried in the Sun's heat!

As more and more people are born on our planet, we use up more and more of our power resources, such as gas, coal and oil. But the Sun is an unlimited resource. Studying the Sun helps us learn how we can use its power. Perhaps one day you'll be one of the scientists who learns how to harness the energy of the Sun to power everything on Earth.

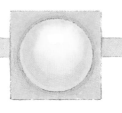

Glossary

absorb: to soak up

astronomer: a scientist who studies the stars, planets and other objects in space

atmosphere: the blanket of gases that surrounds the Earth

core: the innermost part of a planet, moon or star

corona: the glowing layer of gas around the Sun

equator: the imaginary line that goes around the middle of the Earth

equinox: the first day of spring or fall. On these days the Sun is exactly above the equator, and day and night are both 12 hours long.

galaxy: a collection of hundreds of billions of stars, dust, space rocks and gas. Earth is in the Milky Way galaxy.

gas: a form of matter made up of tiny particles that are not connected to each other and so can move freely in space. Air is made up of gases.

gravity: the invisible force that holds everything on Earth, keeps the Moon circling the Earth and holds the Earth and planets around the Sun

hemisphere: half of the Earth's surface. North America is in the Northern hemisphere.

observatory: a place with telescopes and other instruments for studying space

orbit: the path an object takes through space

planet: a large object that circles a star and does not make its own light. Earth is a planet.

rainbow: a band of color you can see in the sky opposite the sun, especially after there has been rain

reflect: to bounce back light (Objects can also reflect heat and sound.)

satellite: a small object that circles a larger body, such as the Moon circling the Earth or a communications satellite circling the Earth

scientist: a person who studies science

solar: about the Sun

solar eclipse: takes place when the Sun, Moon and Earth are in a direct line with the Moon in the middle. The Moon blocks the light of the Sun and the Sun seems to turn dark.

solar system: the Sun and all the objects that orbit it

solstice: one of the two times of the year when the Sun is farthest from the Earth's equator

spacecraft: a vehicle that can travel beyond Earth's atmosphere

star: a ball of burning gas that gives off light

universe: everything, including Earth, in space